20 Forex
(5 Minute Time Frame)

By Thomas Carter

Copyright ©2014 Thomas Carter
thomascarterbook.blogspot.com

All right reserved. No part of this book may be produced or transmitted in any form or by any means, electronic or mechanical, including photocopying, recording, or any information storage and retrieval system, without prior written permission of the author.

DISCLAIMER

Trading forex and other on-exchange and over-the-counter products carries a high level of risk and may not be suitable for all investors. The high degree of leverage associated with such trading can result in losses, as well as gains. the past performance of any trading strategy or methodology is not indicative of future results, which can vary due to market volatility; it should not be interpreted as a forecast of future performance You should carefully consider whether such trading is suitable for you in light of your financial condition, level of experience and appetite for risk and seek advice from independent financial adviser, if you have any doubts.

Table of Contents

DISCLAIMER..2

5 Min Trading System # 1..4

5 Min Trading system # 2..6

5 Min Trading System # 3..7

5 Min Trading System # 4..8

5 Min Trading System # 5..9

5 Min Trading System # 6..12

5 Min Trading System # 7..14

5 Min Trading System # 8..15

5 Min Trading System # 9..16

5 Min Trading System # 10..18

5 Min Trading System # 11..19

5 Min Trading System # 12..21

5 Min Trading System # 13..23

5 Min Trading System # 14..25

5 Min Trading System # 15..27

5 Min Trading System # 16..29

5 Min Trading System # 17..30

5 Min Trading System # 18..32

5 Min Trading System # 19..34

5 Min Trading System # 20..35

FINAL WORDS..36

DOWNLOAD INDICATORS..37

5 Min Trading System # 1

Pair:
EUR/USD

Indicators:
MACD (12,26,1)

Stochastic (5,3,3)

EMA 5 to the close

EMA 5 to the open

Buy Signal:

- When the stochastic crosses up from the 20 line and is not overbought
- The MACD closses higher than the previous time interval
- The signal candle closes higher bullish
- The 5 EMA to the close has crossed the 5 EMA to the open

Stop loss is 20 pips

Close when the 5 EMA to the close has crossed the 5 EMA to the open

Sell Signal

- When the stochastic crosses down from the 80 line and is not oversold

- The MACD closses lower than the previous time interval
- The signal candle closes lower bearish
- The 5 EMA to the close has crossed the 5 EMA to the open

Stop loss is 20 pips

Close when the 5 EMA to the close has crossed the 5 EMA to the open

5 Min Trading system # 2

Pairs:
EUR/USD

Indicators:
10 EMA

21 EMA

50 EMA

System Rules:

- Wait for a trend to shown on the 5 min chart, higher highs in an up trend and lower low in a down trend, look at the 50 EMA for trend strength and direction.

- Make sure you are not in the Asian session or at the end of the London or US session.

- Check there is no major upcoming news about to come out before you place a trade.

- Once price enters into the ZONE, wait for the pullback and open a trade, sell for down trend and buy for up trend.

- Set stop loss at 5 pips + spread

- Set take profit at 10 pips

ZONE is the area between 10 EMA and 21 EMA. The 50 EMA is our gauge for the strength of the trend, in a good strong trend it should be pointing up or down at about 30 degrees from horizontal.

5 Min Trading System # 3

Pairs:
EUR/USD, GBP/USD, USD/JPY, USD/CHF

Indicators:
Bollinger Band (20,2)

Stochastic (5,3,3)

Trading Rules:

- A close must happen outside the bollinger band.
- Stochastic oscillator must be in oversold area (below 20) or overbought area (above 80)
- If market is in uptrend, look for a red candle. If market is in a downtrend, look for a green candle. We will call these the "signal candle".
- Once you see your signal candle, enter in that same direction and aim for 10 pips.
- Stop loss at 20 pips or according to your trading rules.

5 Min Trading System # 4

Pairs:
EUR/USD, GBP/USD, GBP/JPY

Indicators:
Bollinger Band (20,2)

Rules For Long Trades:
- Bollinger band must slope up
- Go long when the price touches the middle bollinger band from above
- Stop loss at lower band or 15 pip
- Take profit at upper band

Rules For Short Trades:
- Bollinger band must slope down
- Go short when the price touches the middle bollinger band from below
- Stop loss at upper band or 15 min
- Take profit at lower band.

5 Min Trading System # 5

Pairs:
Any

Indicators:
3 period EMA shifted 1 (Yellow – dot)
5 period EMA shifted 3 (Dodger Blue – solid – thickness 2)
15 period EMA shifted 3 (Red – solid – thickness 1)
45 period EMA shifted 3 (Grey – dashed)
GHL (Gain Hi Lo)
QTI (Quick Trend Index)

How To Trade:
This system is using a Multi Time Frame System. We are going to use higher time frame to find a setup (15 min) and then drop down to a lower time frame (5 min) to look for the actual trade.

Long Trade Setup:
Step 1 – On the higher time frame, the moving averages and the histograms must all be in alignment.

On the higher time frame:

Price is over the 3 EMA

3 EMA over the 5 EMA

5 EMA over the 15 EMA

15 EMA over the 45 EMA

GHL green

QTI green

Step 2 – On the higher time frame, price must pullback to touch the 5 EMA shifted **3**.

After price touches the 5 EMA, the 3 EMA is likely to drop below the 5 EMA, this is ok ! As long as the 5 EMA remains over the 15 EMA and the 15 EMA remains over the 45 EMA, we are still good to go. The candle that touches the 5 EMA doesn't have to close. In an uptrend, the candle that touches the 5 EMA will be a red bear candle.

Step 3 – Immediately switch to the lower time frame

As soon as the price touches the 5 EMA on the higher time frame, we immediately drop down to the lower time frame This is the time frame we are trading.

Step 4 – On the lower time frame, wait for a buy signal.

There are 4 aspects to a buy signal:

- Price closes above all the moving averages
- The 15 EMA is above the 45 EMA
- Both histograms are green
- The higher time frame is still bullish (moving averages still in the right order and the histograms are still green). When the higher time frame and everything is still looking good, we can place a market order at the close of the entry candle.

Step 5 – On the lower time frame, determine stop loss placement and profit target.

Place stop loss below the recent swing low. Profit target is the same as stop loss. Reward to risk ratio is 1:1

Short Trade Setup:

Step 1 – On the higher time frame, the moving averages and the histograms must all be in alignment.

Price is below the 3 EMA

3 EMA under the 5 EMA

5 EMA under the 15 EMA

15 EMA under the 45 EMA

GHL red

QTI red

Step 2 – On the higher time frame, price must pullback to touch the 5 EMA shifted 3

Step 3 – Immediately switch to the lower time frame

Step 4 – On the lower time frame, wait for a sell signal.

There are 4 aspects to a sell signal:

- Price closes below all the moving averages
- The 15 EMA is under the 45 EMA
- Both histograms are red
- The higher time frame is still bearish (moving averages still in the right order and the histograms are still red). When the higher time frame and everything is still looking good, we can place a market order at the close of the entry candle.

Step 5 – On the lower time frame, determine stop loss placement and profit target.

Place stop loss above the recent swing high. Profit target is the same as stop loss. Reward to risk ratio is 1:1

5 Min Trading System # 6

Pairs:

EUR/USD

Setup

This forex strategy requires 2 charts open simultaneously. Remember to wait till the previous 5 minute bar closes before placing a trade, or closing any open trades.

5 minute chart:

- EMA (14)
- EMA (21)
- EMA (50)
- Bollinger Bands (20, 20)

1 hour chart:

- EMA (14)
- EMA (21)
- EMA (50)
- Bollinger Bands (20, 20)

BUY Entry

5 minute chart:

- EMA (14) > EMA (21)
- EMA (21) > EMA (50)
- EMA (50) is within the Bollinger Bands

1 hour chart:

- EMA (14) > EMA (21)
- EMA (21) > EMA (50)

- EMA (50) is within the Bollinger Bands
- Current bar is touching EMA (14) or EMA (21)
- Current bar closing price is above opening price

Place a BUY trade if all the above conditions are met on both the 5 minute chart and 1 hour chart. Wait for the 5 minute bar to close before taking the trade.

SELL Entry

5 minute chart:

- EMA (14) < EMA (21)
- EMA (21) < EMA (50)
- EMA (50) is within the Bollinger Bands

1 hour chart:

- EMA (14) < EMA (21)
- EMA (21) < EMA (50)
- EMA (50) is within the Bollinger Bands
- Current bar is touching EMA (14) or EMA (21)
- Current bar closing price is below opening price

Place a SELL trade if all the above conditions are met on both the 5 minute chart and 1 hour chart. Wait for the 5 minute bar to close before taking the trade.

Exit

Exit the trade if the following conditions are <u>no longer</u> met on both the 5 minute and 1 hour chart:

- EMA (14) > EMA (21) > EMA (50) for buy trade.
- EMA (14) < EMA (21) < EMA (50) for sell trade.
- EMA (50) is within the Bollinger Bands

5 Min Trading System # 7

Pairs

This method works best with volatile pairs such as GBPJPY, or GBPUSD.

Setup

At 08:00 EST (New York Time), draw a box enclosing the high and low of the previous hour.

Entry

BUY if the price moves above the box by 20% of the box height. SELL if the price moves below the box by 20% of the box height. This signal is only valid for one hour after it is generated.

Exit

Close the BUY trade when the price hits 400% above the box height. Close the SELL trade when the price hits 400% below the box height.

Initial stop loss for the BUY trade is the bottom of the box.
Initial stop loss for the SELL trade is the top of the box.

Place a trailing stop equivalent to the size of the box to capture the profits gained.

5 Min Trading System # 8

Pairs:
Any

Indicators:
Bollinger Bands:

Period 50, Deviations 2 – Red

Period 50, Deviations 3 – Yellow

Period 50, Deviations 4 – Orange

RSI with period 3

Stochastic (6,3,3)

Long Entry:
Wait for the candle to touch or penetrate the Red Bollinger Band. The RSI should be below 20 now. So would the stochastic. If the next candle retrace back through the Red Bollinger Band, the RSI falls above the 20 level and the stochastic crosses lines (above or just 40) you put in a buy order.

Sell Entry:
Wait for the candle to touch or penetrate the Red Bollinger Band. The RSI should be above 80 now. So would the stochastic. If the next candle retrace back through the Red Bollinger Band, the RSI falls below the 80 level and the stochastic crosses lines (just below 60) you put in a sell order.

Exit:
Stop loss on Yellow or Orange Band. Take profit on middle band.

5 Min Trading System # 9

Pairs:
Any

Indicators:
50 EMA

100 EMA

MACD (12,26,9)

Long Trades:

- Wait for the currency to trade above both the 50 EMA and 100 EMA
- Once the price has broken above the 50 EMA by 10 pips or more enter long if MACD crosses to positive within the last five bars, otherwise wait for the next MACD signal.
- Initial stop set at five bar low from entry.
- Exit half of the position at two times risk; move stop to breakeven.
- Exit second half when price breaks below 50 EMA by 10 pips.
- Do not take the trade if the price is simply trading between the 50 and 100 EMA.

Short Trades:

- Wait for the currency to trade below both the 50 EMA and 100 EMA.
- Once the price has broken below the 50 EMA by 10 pips or

more enter short if MACD crosses to negative within the last five bars; otherwise wait for next MACD signal.

- Initial stop set at five bar high from entry.
- Exit half of the position at two times risk, move the stop to breakeven.
- Exit remaining position when the price breaks back above the 50 EMA by 10 pips.
- Do not take the trade if the price is simply trading between the 50 and 100 EMA.

5 Min Trading System # 10

Pairs:
Any

Indicators:
40 EMA

80 EMA

CCI (21)

Rules:
We only buy if the 40 EMA is above the 80 EMA and we only sell if the 40 EMA is below the 80 EMA. If the 40 EMA is above the 80 EMA we look to buy when the CCI indicators crosses from below 0.0 to above 0.0. If the 40 EMA is below the 80 EMA we look to sell when the CCI indicators crosses from above 0.0 to below 0.0

Stop Loss
10 – 15 pips

Take Profit
10 – 15 pips

5 Min Trading System # 11

Pairs:

Any

Indicators:

5 EMA

10 EMA

RSI (14)

Stochastic (5,3,3)

MACD (12,26,9)

BUY:

Open 4H chart:

if 5 EMA above 10 EMA, trend is up

Open 5 min / 15 min chart:

5 EMA must cross above the 10 EMA

RSI > 50

Stochastic must be headed up and not in overbought territory

MACD histogram must go from negative to positive or MACD histograms must be negative and start to increase value.

SELL:

Open 4H chart:

if 5 EMA below 10 EMA, trend is down

Open 5 min / 15 min chart:

5 EMA must cross below the 10 EMA

RSI < 50

Stochastic must be headed down and not in oversold territory

MACD histograms must go from positive to negative or MACD histograms must be positive and start to decrease value.

Stop Loss and Profit Target:

Stop Loss = 20 - 30 pips

Profit Target = 20 - 30 pips

5 Min Trading System # 12

Pairs:
Any

Indicators:
16 EMA

48 EMA

Laquerre

Long Entry:
- The closing price is stay above the 16 EMA
- The 16 EMA stay above the 48 EMA
- Laquerre cuts above 0.8 level

Stop Loss:
30 pips below the entry point

Profit Target:
20 – 30 pips

Short Entry:
- The closing price is stay below the 16 EMA
- The 16 EMA stay below the 48 EMA
- Laquerre cuts below 0.2 level

Stop Loss:
30 pips above the entry point

Profit Target:
20 – 30 pips

5 Min Trading System # 13

Pairs:
EUR/USD
GBP/USD

Indicators:
CCI (14)
MACD (12,26,9)

Long Entry
CCI crosses +100 from BELOW (meaning CCI has to enter the overbought zone)

MACD moving average has to be below the histogram

MACD histograms bar needs to have a higher value than the previous bar.

Short Entry
CCI crosses -100 from ABOVE (meaning CCI has to enter the oversold zone)

MACD moving average has to be above the histogram

MACD histograms bar needs to have a lower value than the previous bar.

Stop Loss:
12 – 15 pips

Profit Target:

AUD/USD => 7 pips

EUR/USD => 8 pips

GBP/USD => 10 pips

5 Min Trading System # 14

Pairs:
Any

Indicators:
10 WMA

20 SMA

Slow Stochastic (10,6,6) exponential

RSI (28)

MACD (24,52,18)

Buy Rules:
- 10 WMA > 20 SMA
- Stochastic is signaling up (fast line above the slow line)
- RSI > 50
- MACD > 0

Sell Rules:
- 10 WMA < 20 SMA
- Stochastic is signaling down (fast line below slow line)
- RSI < 50
- MACD < 0

Stop Loss:
recent swing high / low

Profit Target:
same as stop loss

5 Min Trading System # 15

Pairs:
Any

Indicators:
15 EMA
50 EMA High
50 EMA Low
MACD (15,70,1,24)

Long Trade Rules:
- 15 EMA is above the 50 EMA channel
- MACD is green
- There is a green arrow

Short Trade Rules:
- 15 EMA is below the 50 EMA channel
- MACD is red
- There is a red arrow

Stop Loss
recent swing high / low

Profit Target
Same as stop loss

Note:

Many times there are good signals when the 15 EMA is just inside the 50 EMA channel. Practice to recognize when it's okay to take trades when the 15 EMA is inside the 50 EMA channel.

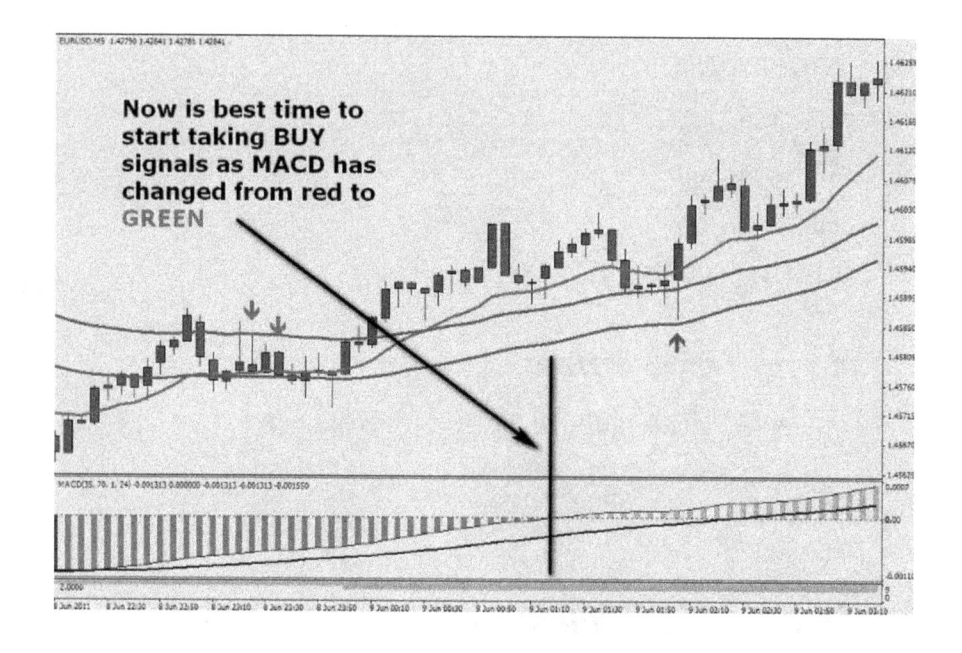

5 Min Trading System # 16

Pairs:
EUR/USD
GBP/USD
AUD/USD
USD/CHF

Indicators:
Directional Movement Index (ADX) => setting: (DI+, DI-, 14 periods)

5 Weight Moving Average (close)

11 Simple Moving Average (close)

Parabolic Sar (0.1, 0.01)

Long Entry:
5 WMA > 11 SMA

Parabolic Sar below the candles

ADX DI+ > DI-

Short Entry:
5 WMA < 11 SMA

Parabolic Sar above the candles

ADX DI- > DI+

Exit and Stop
Exit => Parabolic Sar signal in opposite direction or at your

discretion.

Stop => previous swing high / low

5 Min Trading System # 17

Pairs:

Major Pair

Indicators:

3 EMA (aqua)

8 EMA (yellow)

MACD (12,26,9)

Stochastic (10,15,15)

Parabolic SAR (0.02, 0.2)

SD (20)

RSI (9)

IMPORTANT ! Pay attention to value of Standard Deviation (20):

AUD & NZD Pairs:

0.0001 – 0.0005 => weak

0.0005 – 0.0010 => medium

>= 0.0010 => strong

JPY Pairs:

0.05 – 0.10 => weak

0.10 – 0.20 => medium

>= 0.20 => strong

Other Pairs:

0.005 – 0.010 => weak

0.010 – 0.020 => medium

>= 0.020 => strong

Rules For Long Trade:

3 EMA > 8 EMA

Parabolic SAR below the candle

MACD > 0

Stochastic: blue line cross up red line

Standard Deviation in medium or strong market.

If all conditions are met => open buy position.

Close position if 3 EMA < 8 EMA

Stop Loss at recent swing low

Rules For Short Trade:

3 EMA < 8 EMA

Parabolic SAR above the candle

MACD < 0

Stochastic: blue line cross down red line

Standard Deviation in medium or strong market.

If all conditions are met => open sell position.

Close position if 3 EMA > 8 EMA

Stop Loss at recent swing high

5 Min Trading System # 18

Pairs:
Any

Indicators:
20 EMA

MACD (12,26,9)

Rules for a long trade:
1. Look for currency pair trading below the 20 EMA and MACD to be negative.
2. Wait for the price to cross above the 20 EMA then make sure that MACD is either in the process of crossing from negative to positive or has crossed into positive territory no longer than five bars ago.
3. Go long 10 pips above the 20 EMA.
4. For an aggressive trade, place a stop loss at the swing low on the five minute chart. For a conservative trade, place a stop 20 pips below the 20 EMA.
5. Sell half of the position at entry plus the amount risked, move the stop on the second half to breakeven.
6. Trail the stop by 20 EMA minus 15 pips.

Rules for short trade:
1. Look for currency pair trading above the 20 EMA and MACD to be positive.
2. Wait for the price to cross below the 20 EMA then make sure that MACD is either in the process of crossing from positive to negative or has crossed into negative territory no longer

than five bars ago.

3. Go short 10 pips below the 20 EMA.
4. For an aggressive trade, place a stop loss at the swing high on the five minute chart. For a conservative trade, place a stop 20 pips above the 20 EMA.
5. Sell half of the position at entry plus the amount risked, move the stop on the second half to breakeven.
6. Trail the stop by 20 EMA minus 15 pips.

5 Min Trading System # 19

Pairs:

EUR/USD

GBP/USD

AUD/USD

Indicators:

Parabolic Sar (0.01-0.01)

MACD colored (64,128,9)

100 EMA

Long Entry:

When the price is above the 100 EMA and Parabolic Sar is up and MACD > 0

Short Entry:

When the price is below the 100 EMA and Parabolic Sar is down and MACD < 0

Stop Loss:

Place stop loss 3 pips below / above the first Parabolic Sar dot.

Take Profit:

7 – 12 pips or better

5 Min Trading System # 20

Pairs:
Any

Indicators:
3 EMA
Bollinger Band (20,3)
MACD (12,26,9)

Enter Long:
When the 3 EMA has crossed up through the middle band at the same time, MACD should be approaching or crossing its zero line going up.

Enter Short:
When the 3 EMA has crossed down through the middle band at the same time, MACD should be approaching or crossing its zero line going down.

Stop Loss:
10 – 15 pips

Target profit:
10 – 15 pips

FINAL WORDS

Thank you for downloading this book. I hope this book was able to help you to jump start your forex trading adventure. If you enjoyed this book, please take the time to share your thoughts and post a review on amazon. It's be greatly appreciated !

I wish you all the best with trading,

Thomas Carter

DOWNLOAD INDICATORS

Indicators can be downloaded at

thomascarterbook.blogspot.com